Ways into Science

Habitats

Peter Riley

W
FRANKLIN WATTS
LONDON • SYDNEY

First published in 2014 by
Franklin Watts
338 Euston Road
London NW1 3BH

Franklin Watts Australia
Level 17/207 Kent Street
Sydney NSW 2000

HB ISBN: 978 1 4451 3475 8
Library eBook ISBN: 978 1 4451 3844 2
Dewey classification number: 620.1

Editor: Julia Bird
Designer: Basement 68

Photo acknowledgements:
All photography Roy Moller except: Aggata /Dreamstime:
15c. Kalinina Alisa/Shutterstock: 9b. Martynova Anna/
Shutterstock: 7t. B1e2n3i4/Dreamstime: 13tl. Radu Bercan/
Shutterstock: 20c. BM Productions/Shutterstock: 5tr, 14b.
Steve Byland/Shutterstock: 3, 9t. Bonita Cheshier/
Dreamstime: 11b. Mohammed Anwarul Kabir Choudhury/
Dreamstime: 10. Antonio Clemens/Dreamstime: 22b.
Blanchi de Costela/Dreamstime: 4, 11t. Melinda Fawver/
Dreamstime: 17tr, 28cl. Andrew Fletcher/Shutterstock: 8b.
Martin Good/istock: 12t, 13tc. Eric Isselee/Shutterstock: 24cr,
26b. Mny-Jhee/Shutterstock: 21t. Sarah Cheriton-Jones/
Shutterstock: 23. Andrew F Kazmierski/Dreamstime: 18.
D Kucharski K Kucharska/Shutterstock: 20bl. Holly Kuchera/
Dreamstime: 6. Limpopoboy/Dreamstime: 5br, 13cr. Madlen/
Shutterstock: 7bl. Krzysztof Odziomek/Shutterstock: 24cl.
Ryan Pike/Dreamstime: 17cr, 28br. Reiza/Shutterstock: 7br.
Ryan Sartoski/Dreamstime: 24br. Seesea/Dreamstime: 15t.
Shevs/Dreamstime: front cover t. Conny Sjostrom/
Shutterstock: 5crb, 8t. Christopher Smith/Dreamstime: 13bl.
Anton Starikov/Dreamstime: 17cl, 28cr. Andrzej Tokarski/
Dreamstime: 5bl, 17tl. Urospoteko/Dreamstime: 12b, 13tr.
Hector Ruiz Villar/Shutterstock: 5cr, 24bl. Kirsanov Valeriy
Vladimirovich/Shutterstock: 20br, 28bl. Barrie Watts: front
cover b. Shaun Wilkinson/Shutterstock: 20t, 30.
Every attempt has been made to clear copyright.
Should there be any inadvertent omission,
please apply to the Publishers for rectification.

Printed in China

Franklin Watts is a division of
Hachette Children's Books,
an Hachette UK company.
www.hachette.co.uk

Contents

What is a **living thing?**

There are seven ways to tell if something is living. These are easy to see when we look at animals.

It moves.

It grows.

It breathes.

It feeds.

It is sensitive.

It has young.

It gets rid of waste.

They are more difficult to see when we look at plants.

A plant is sensitive to light. It moves as it grows towards the light.

It uses light to make food in its leaves.

It feeds by taking up minerals in the soil.

It breathes through tiny holes in its leaves.

It has young (seeds).

It gets rid of waste in its dead leaves.

What do we call the place where plants and animals live? Turn the page to find out.

Habitats

Plants and animals live in habitats.

Some plants and animals live in grassy places, like this field.

Some live in stony places.

8

Trees are home to living things as well.

This pond is full of living things.

Different living things like to live in different habitats.

Plants in a habitat

Plants need soil and light in their habitats.

The plant's roots hold it in the soil.

Plants need water and minerals from the soil. They take them up in their roots.

roots →

Plants need light to make food.

Some plants need lots of light.

Some plants only need dim light.

What do animals need in their habitats? Turn the page to find out.

Animals in a habitat

Animals need food in their habitats. Some animals eat plants. They are called herbivores.

Some animals eat other animals. They are called carnivores.

Animals can be linked together to form a food chain.

A producer
of food

A herbivore

A carnivore

Animals also need shelter in their habitats.

Some animals use materials to make their nests.

13

A grassy habitat

Lots of plants live in a grassy place like this lawn.

Look at a lawn. Can you see the plants shown here?

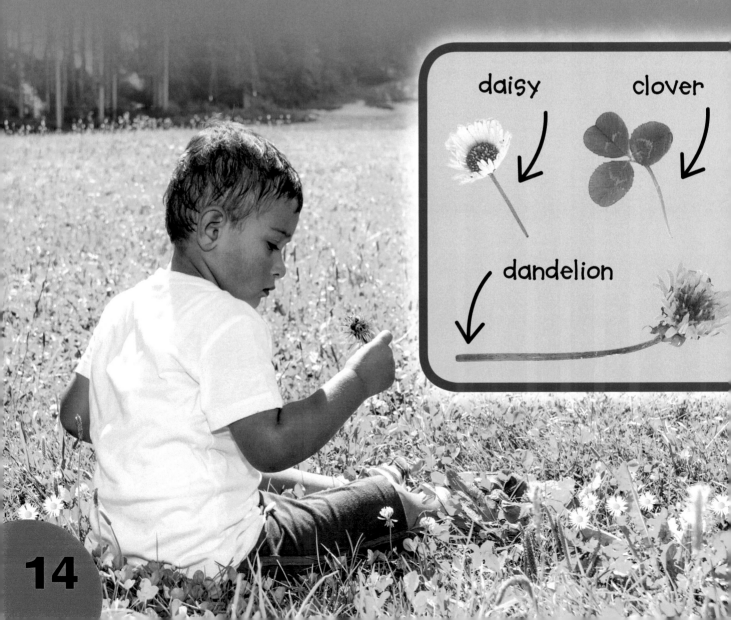

daisy

clover

dandelion

Some animals live in grassy places, too.

Ground beetles live in damp grass.

A harvestman lives in tall grass. It has eight long, thin legs like a spider.

Look closely at a lawn. Can you see any little animals?

15

A stony habitat

Sometimes there is soil in the cracks between stones.

Some plants can grow there.

Can you find plants in cracks between stones?

Some animals live under stones.

You can see them by turning over a stone.

Here are some of the animals you may find.

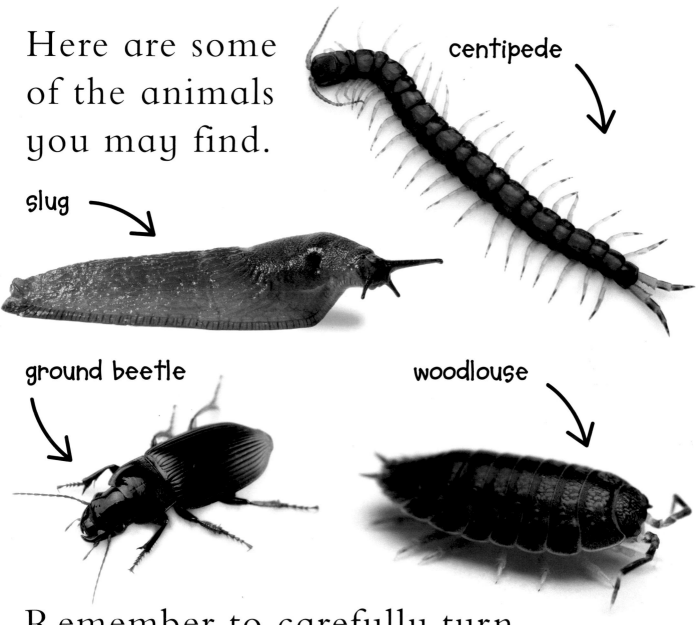

centipede

slug

ground beetle

woodlouse

Remember to carefully turn the stone back over again.

Cracks and spaces under stones are little places to live. They are called micro habitats.

A tree

A tree is
a habitat
for other
living things.

Ivy plants
grow on
tree trunks.

Moss plants live
on damp bark.

Raj wants to see what animals are living on a branch.

He puts a white sheet under a branch. He shakes the branch.

What does Raj see? Turn the page to find out.

On a branch

Raj sees spiders, aphids, weevils and caterpillars.

spider

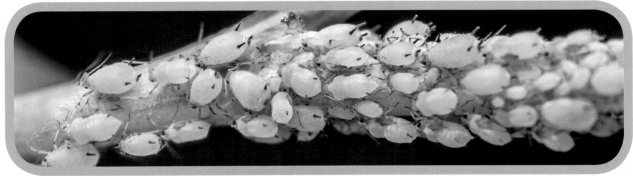

aphids

weevil

caterpillar

Raj empties the sheet close to the tree so the animals can go back to it.

Try the branch test. What do you find?

20

Under a tree

Some trees lose their leaves in the autumn.

The fallen leaves are called leaf litter.

Leaf litter is a home for some animals.

Hannah collects some leaf litter.

21

Hannah empties the bag onto a white sheet.

She moves the leaves apart.

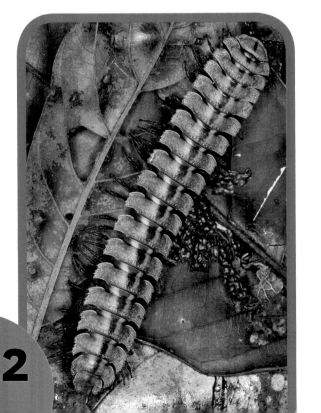

Hannah finds some millipedes.

She puts the leaves and animals back where she found them.

The pond habitat

Lots of animals and plants live in or around a pond.

What animals do you think you might find in this pond? Make a list and then turn the page to find out.

Pond **creatures**

Here are some animals that live in a pond.

fish

pond snail

water beetle

tadpole

Matthew is making a home for pond snails.

Make a home for pond snails. Look at them every day. What do you find out?

He puts gravel in the bottom of a tank.

He puts water plants in the gravel.

He pours in some water and puts in the snails.

25

Habitat survey

Paul is doing a survey about animals in a stony habitat.

He turns over five stones and looks at the animals living under them.

He records his results in a table.

Animal	Stone 1	2	3	4	5	Total
Woodlouse	1	?	?	?	?	?
Earthworm	1	?	?	?	?	?
Beetle	2	?	?	?	?	?
Spider	0	?	?	?	?	?
Snail	0	?	?	?	?	?

Try this survey for yourself.

Nicole is doing a survey about plants in a grassy habitat.

She throws a hoop to five different places on a lawn.

She records the plants she sees inside the hoop each time.

Plant	Hoop 1	2	3	4	5	Total
Grass	1	?	?	?	?	?
Buttercup	1	?	?	?	?	?
Daisy	3	?	?	?	?	?
Dandelion	0	?	?	?	?	?
Thistle	0	?	?	?	?	?

Try this survey for yourself.

27

Useful words

Aphid – a small insect that eats plants.

Bark – a covering on the trunk, branches and twigs of trees and bushes.

Branch – a side shoot from the trunk of a tree or bush.

Centipede – animal with a long body divided into parts called segments. Each segment has a pair of legs.

Food chain – a way of showing how plants and animals are linked together by the way they feed.

Gravel – small stones that can be used in aquarium tanks to hold water plants in place.

Micro habitat – a small place where things live such as under a leaf, a stone or a log.

Millipede – an animal with a long body divided into many segments, with covers over the segments. Each cover has two pairs of legs.

Minerals – food that plants take from the soil.

Sensitive – able to sense things such as noise and light in the surroundings.

Soil – a mixture of tiny pieces of rock, dead plants and animals.

Some answers

Here are some answers to the questions we have asked in this book. Don't worry if you had some different answers to ours: you may be right too. Talk through your answers with other people and see if you can explain why they are right.

Page 15 If the lawn is wet you may find slugs and snails or an earthworm. In dry weather you may see a spider or a beetle or, particularly in the autumn, a harvestman. If there are plants in flower on the lawn you may find bees visiting them.

Page 20 If you shake a branch you might find aphids, spiders or weevils which are a type of beetle. You may find some caterpillars that move by making their backs rise in an arch. These caterpillars are known as loopers or inchworms and will change into moths.

Page 25 The pond snails will feed on a green slime that grows on the water plants. If slime grows on the glass you can see the snails feeding on it by sticking out their tongues to scrape it off. Snails have tiny teeth on their tongues which break up the slime.

Pages 26 and 27 The number of animals under each stone will vary. You may find more animals under damp stones than dry ones. Some plants such as buttercups and clover spread their leaves and flowers. You may have to look down to where the stem goes into the soil to find out how many plants are there.

Index

About this book

Ways into Science is designed to encourage children to think about their everyday world in a scientific way and to make investigations to test their ideas. There are five lines of enquiry that scientists make in investigations. These are grouping and classifying, observing over time, making a fair test, searching for patterns and researching using secondary sources.

• When children open this book they are already making one line of enquiry – researching habitats. As they read through the book they are invited to make other lines of enquiry and to develop skills in scientific investigation.

• On page 15 they are invited to try out their observational skills.

• On pages 19 and 23 they are asked to make a prediction.

• On pages 20 and 22 they are asked to perform a simple test, observe closely and to group and classify.

• On page 25 they are asked to make observations over time.

• On pages 26 and 27 they are asked to perform simple tests, observe closely, group and classify, gather and record data.